WHERE'S WALLY?
IN
HOLLYWOOD
DELUXE EDITION

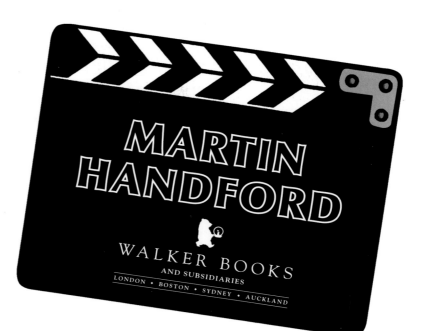

MARTIN HANDFORD

WALKER BOOKS
AND SUBSIDIARIES
LONDON • BOSTON • SYDNEY • AUCKLAND

A DREAM COME TRUE

WOW, WALLY-WATCHERS, THIS IS FANTASTIC, I'M REALLY IN HOLLYWOOD! LOOK AT THE FILM PEOPLE EVERYWHERE – I WONDER WHAT MOVIES THEY'RE MAKING. THIS IS MY DREAM COME TRUE ... TO MEET THE DIRECTORS AND ACTORS, TO WALK THROUGH THE CROWDS OF EXTRAS, TO SEE BEHIND THE SCENES! PHEW, I WONDER IF I'LL APPEAR IN A MOVIE MYSELF!

★ ★ ★ ★ WHAT TO LOOK FOR IN HOLLYWOOD! ★ ★ ★ ★

WELCOME TO TINSELTOWN, WALLY-WATCHERS! THESE ARE THE PEOPLE AND THINGS TO LOOK FOR AS YOU WALK THROUGH THE FILM SETS WITH WALLY.

★ FIRST (OF COURSE!) WHERE'S WALLY?

★ NEXT FIND WALLY'S CANINE COMPANION, WOOF – REMEMBER, ALL YOU CAN SEE IS HIS TAIL!

★ THEN FIND WALLY'S FRIEND, WENDA!

★ ABRACADABRA! NOW FOCUS IN ON WIZARD WHITEBEARD!

★ BOO! HISS! HERE COMES THE BAD GUY, ODLAW!

★ NOW SPOT THESE 25 WALLY-WATCHERS, EACH OF WHOM APPEARS ONLY ONCE BEFORE THE FINAL FANTASTIC SCENE!

★ WOW! INCREDIBLE! SPOT ONE OTHER CHARACTER WHO APPEARS IN EVERY SCENE EXCEPT THE LAST!

★ ★ KEEP ON SEARCHING! THERE'S MORE TO FIND! ★ ★

ON EVERY SET, FIND WALLY'S LOST KEY!
WOOF'S LOST BONE! WENDA'S LOST CAMERA! WIZARD WHITEBEARD'S SCROLL!
ODLAW'S LOST BINOCULARS! AND A MISSING CAN OF FILM!

★ ★ ★ ★ ★ ★ ★ AND MORE AND MORE! ★ ★ ★ ★ ★ ★ ★

EACH OF THE FOUR POSTERS ON THE WALL OVER THERE IS PART OF ONE OF THE FILM SETS WALLY IS ABOUT TO VISIT. ★ FIND OUT WHERE THE POSTERS CAME FROM. ★ THEN SPOT ANY DIFFERENCES BETWEEN THE POSTERS AND THE SETS.

CHECKLIST: SHHH! THIS IS A SILENT MOVIE

- A trail of leaking buckets
- A knotted hose
- A tug-of-war
- Some flowers being watered
- A man in plus-four trousers
- Two butterfly catchers
- Nine four-legged animals
- A runaway wheel
- Seven loudhailers
- A watchtower
- Thirteen balloons

- Fifteen movie cameras
- A searchlight
- Three men tripping on some fruit
- A hose cut by an axe
- Four fire chiefs wearing peaked caps
- A railway-track ladder
- Three men wearing red shirts and braces
- Two umbrellas
- A convict lamp stand
- Three runaway flames
- A game of croquet
- Two convicts wearing spots

SHHH! THIS IS A SILENT MOVIE

SO THIS IS HOW THE HOLLYWOOD DREAM BEGAN – WITH SILENT MOVIES MADE IN BLACK AND WHITE. IT LOOKS CRAZY AND IT MAKES YOU LAUGH. ACTING IN SLAPSTICK COMEDIES MUST BE REALLY HARD – LOOK HOW MANY ACCIDENTS ARE HAPPENING. BUT THE GREAT THING IS THAT NONE OF THE ACTORS EVER GET HURT, HOWEVER OFTEN THEY FALL FLAT ON THEIR FACES!

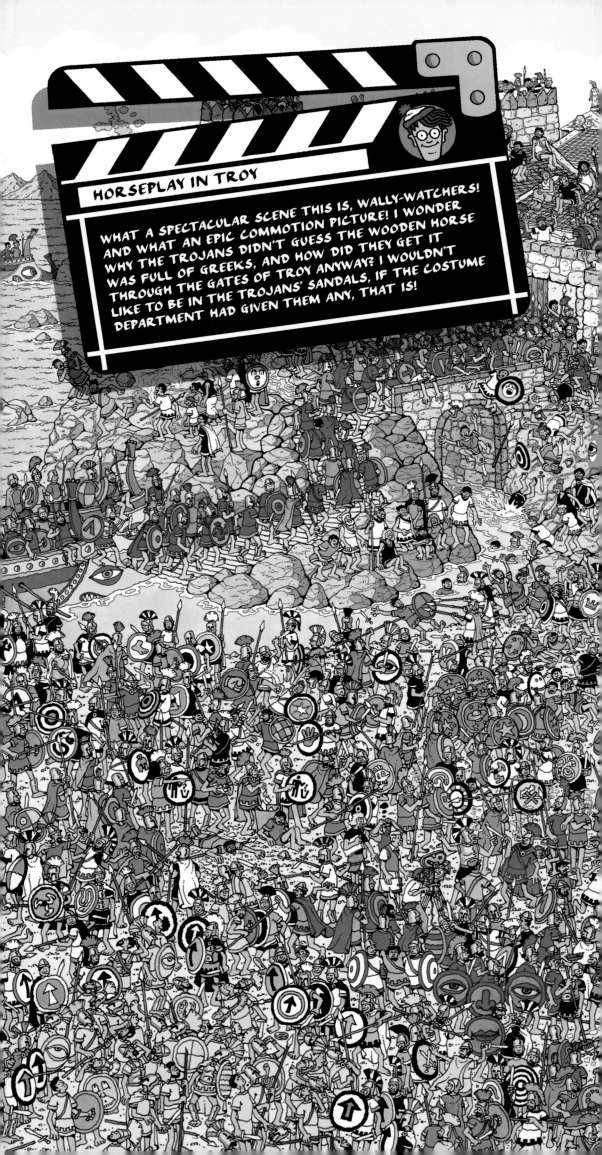

CHECKLIST: HORSEPLAY IN TROY

- Five blue soldiers with red-crested helmets
- Three soldiers with extra-long cloaks
- Thirteen real four-legged animals
- Three film crew members wearing sunglasses
- Five red soldiers with blue-crested helmets
- Five yellow soldiers with blue-crested helmets
- Four statues waving at each other
- A litter bin
- Two broken hearts
- Two soldiers with slings
- Two snaky carvings

- A soldier with a square shield
- Crew members surrendering
- Three Trojans drinking coffee
- Ten arrows that are stuck in shields
- One soldier wearing sandals
- Soldiers arguing about the time
- Some ancient traffic police
- A tumbling waterfall
- Five soldiers with brooms
- Two soldiers sharing a cloak

FUN IN THE FOREIGN LEGION

PHEW, FILM FANS, DON'T GET OVERHEATED, THIS IS THE MOST SIZZLING LOCATION SO FAR! EVERYONE'S SWELTERING, FROM STARS TO SAND-SHIFTERS. SOME OF THOSE EXTRAS LOOK LIKE THEY'RE LOSING THEIR COOL – HAVE THEY FORGOTTEN THIS IS ONLY A FILM? PERHAPS IT'S TIME A FEW MORE OF THEM DESERTED THE DESERT AND JOINED THE RUSH FOR ICE CREAM!

CHECKLIST: A TREMENDOUS SONG AND DANCE

- [ ] One dancer wearing a blue carnation
- [ ] Some tap dancers
- [ ] A "grand" piano
- [ ] A musician playing a double bass
- [ ] Dancers wearing top hat and tails
- [ ] Sailors saluting the ships's "N" sign
- [ ] Sailors with bell-bottom trousers
- [ ] The captain's log
- [ ] A vice admiral
- [ ] A piano keyboard

- [ ] Four orange feathers
- [ ] A soldier on the wrong set
- [ ] Five real anchors
- [ ] An octopus, a shark and a fish
- [ ] Nine mops
- [ ] Four sailors with tattoos
- [ ] Three men sweeping up musical notes
- [ ] A tap dancer in the wrong suit
- [ ] A harp swing
- [ ] Upside-down scenery

A TREMENDOUS SONG AND DANCE

HAVE YOU EVER SEEN SUCH AMAZING MUSICAL MAYHEM? DEFINITELY A DEAFENING SCENE OF NOTE. THAT BATTLESHIP'S STEERING CERTAINLY NEEDS FINE-TUNING! BUT LET'S NOT MAKE TOO MUCH OF A SONG AND DANCE ABOUT IT. EVEN IF ALL THE CAST ARE SWEPT OFF THEIR FEET, THE SHOW MUST GO ON!

CHECKLIST: CAVE OF THE PLUNDERING PIRATES

- [ ] A man asleep in bed
- [ ] A man awake in bed
- [ ] A pirate carrying a grey treasure chest
- [ ] A pirate wearing a blue shoe and a white shoe
- [ ] A pirate wearing a red shoe and a pink shoe
- [ ] A pirate with a red star on his cap
- [ ] A pirate with jewels in his beard
- [ ] A golden bath
- [ ] A snake

- [ ] Two dogs and a horse
- [ ] A "chest" of drawers
- [ ] Three real pirate ghosts
- [ ] A pirate barber
- [ ] Surprised miners
- [ ] Two careless carpet-carriers
- [ ] Pirates stealing camera equipment
- [ ] Two walking pots
- [ ] A pirate wearing a yellow cap
- [ ] Pirates carrying a cannon
- [ ] Two pirates stealing swords
- [ ] A romantic pirate
- [ ] A pirate stealing an earring

CAVE OF THE PLUNDERING PIRATES

WHAT A PLETHORA OF PLUNDERING PIRATES, WALLY-WATCHERS! WHAT A CRUSH IN THE CAVE! THERE MUST BE TONS OF TREATS AND TRINKETS IN THIS TEEMING TREASURE TROVE. WITH SPOOKY SPIRITS CENTRE STAGE AND PIRATICAL PILFERERS TO SPOT, THE DIRECTOR CERTAINLY HAS HIS HANDS FULL. LET'S HOPE HE HAS THE GOLDEN TOUCH! SHIVER-ME-TIMBERS, WHAT A FEARFULLY FUNNY FLICK THIS IS!

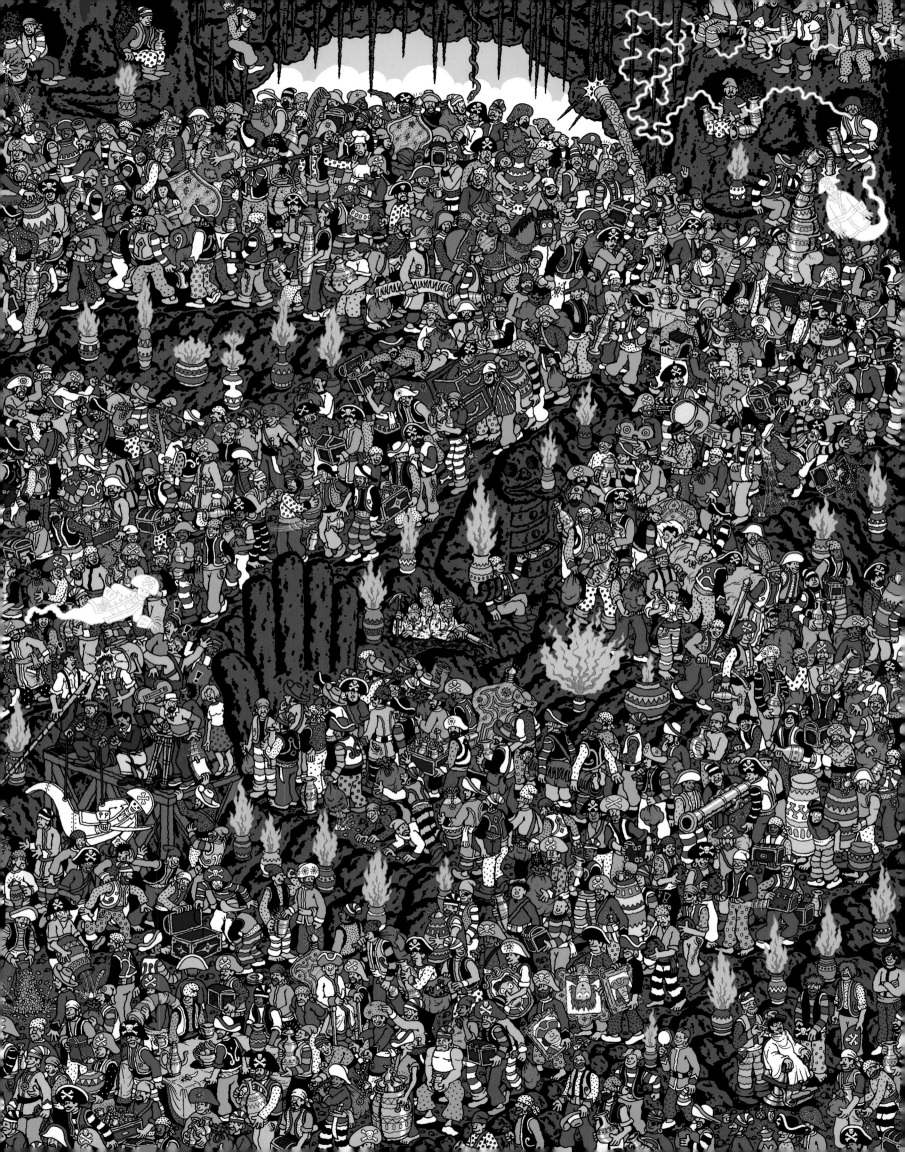

CHECKLIST: THE SWASHBUCKLING MUSKETEERS

- [ ] Eleven gentlemen bowing
- [ ] Two wheelbarrows
- [ ] Twelve spouts of water
- [ ] A tear-jerking emotional scene
- [ ] A gentleman with only one glove
- [ ] Badly dressed men turned away from the dance
- [ ] Three musket tears
- [ ] One lost glove
- [ ] Four real animals

- [ ] A man wearing different coloured gloves
- [ ] A bouncer
- [ ] Three angry gardeners
- [ ] Two swordsmen "fencing"
- [ ] Three mixed-up statues
- [ ] A man having his foot tickled
- [ ] Four ladies being presented with flowers
- [ ] A hat with a striped plume
- [ ] A sad flower-bed
- [ ] An extra-large glove
- [ ] Men green with envy
- [ ] A cat siren
- [ ] Two fuel pumps

THE SWASHBUCKLING MUSKETEERS

ALL FOR ONE, ONE FOR ALL! – WASN'T THAT THE MOTTO OF THE THREE MUSKETEERS? NOW LOOK AT THIS FREE-FOR-ALL! CAN YOU SPOT OUR THREE GALLANT HEROES BATTLING WITH THE RED-COATED CARDINAL'S GUARDS? WITH ALL THIS SWASHBUCKLING ACTION GOING ON, I WONDER HOW THE CAMERAMEN CAN CAPTURE IT ALL ON FILM!

DINOSAURS, SPACEMEN AND GHOULS

PHEW, INCREDIBLE! TIME, SPACE AND HORROR ARE IN A MIGHTY MUDDLE HERE! WHAT COSMIC COSTUMES AND WHAT GREAT SPECIAL EFFECTS! ONE OF THOSE FLYING SAUCERS LOOKS LIKE IT'S REALLY FLYING! ARE THOSE REAL ALIENS INSIDE, NOT ACTORS AT ALL? SO WHAT'S REAL AND WHAT'S MADE UP IN FILMS LIKE THESE?

WHEN THE STARS COME OUT

WOW, WALLY-WATCHERS, THIS IS WHAT I CALL GLAMOUR! I'M AT A MAJOR MOVIE PREMIERE. THE STARS HAVE COME TO SEE THE FILM, THE CROWDS HAVE COME TO SEE THE STARS. LOOK AT THAT PINK STRETCH LIMO – NOW THAT'S A PROPER CAR FOR A STAR. AND WHO'S IN THE BONE-MOBILE BEHIND? AND DOESN'T KING KONG LOOK NICER IN LIFE THAN WHEN HE'S ON THE SCREEN?

WHERE'S WALLY? THE MUSICAL

WOW, WHAT AN EXTRAVAGANZA, WALLY-WATCHERS – THIS ALL-SINGING, ALL-DANCING MOVIE IS ALL ABOUT ME AND MY FRIENDS! LOOK HOW MANY ACTORS ARE DRESSED UP AS ME! AND LOOK AT ALL THE WOOFS, WENDAS, WIZARD WHITEBEARDS AND ODLAWS. HAVE YOU NOTICED THAT THE WARDROBE DEPARTMENT HAS MADE MISTAKES WITH SOME OF THE ACTORS' COSTUMES? BUT THAT WON'T HELP YOU FIND THE REAL ME AND MY FOUR FRIENDS IN THIS FILM! I'LL GIVE YOU SOME CLUES. I'M THE WALLY WITH SOMETHING EXTRA FOR WOOF. ALL YOU CAN SEE OF THE REAL WOOF IS HIS TAIL. THE REAL WENDA HAS A CAMERA. THE REAL WIZARD WHITEBEARD IS WEARING A HAT BENT TO THE LEFT. AND THE REAL ODLAW IS HOLDING A WALKING STICK.

THERE'S JUST ONE MORE THING. I'VE BEEN FOLLOWED HERE BY ONE CHARACTER FROM EVERY SET I'VE VISITED. SO CAN YOU SPOT ALL ELEVEN OF THEM IN THIS SCENE? AND CAN YOU FIND OUT WHEN EACH CHARACTER FIRST JOINED ME; AND CATCH ALL THEIR APPEARANCES THROUGHOUT MY TRAVELS?

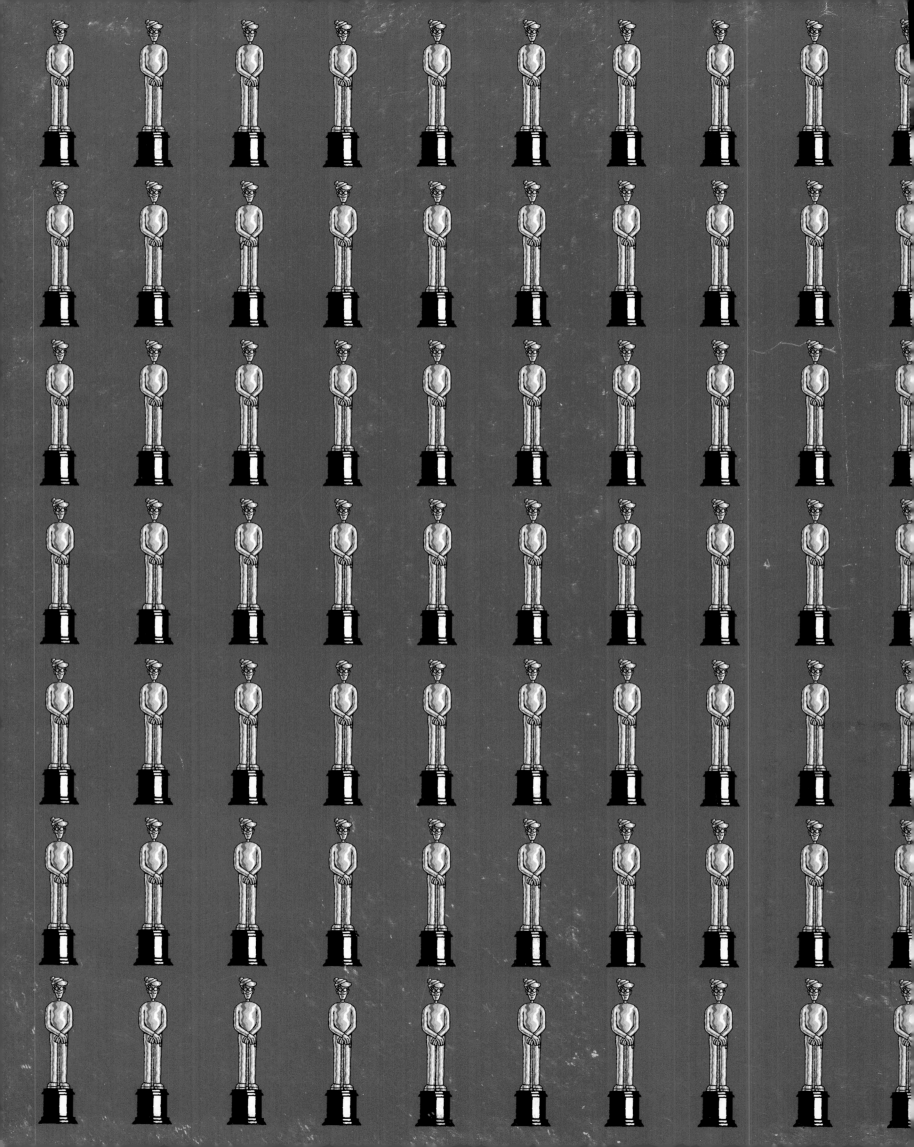